T0055965

The Making of the Drum

Bob Chilcott

for SATB and percussion

In 1984 I was very fortunate to visit Uganda, where a drum maker made me a beautiful drum with a snakeskin head. I'll never forget sitting in the plane to come home and seeing by chance the baggage handlers loading my drum with incredible respect and care. The drum to them is a living spirit.

The poems I set are a celebration of how that spirit is brought to life. The piece enacts the ritual of constructing the drum, whose component parts are drawn from the surrounding nature—a nature that gives of itself almost sacrificially. We hear how the goat is killed for its skin, how the tree, which bleeds cedar-dark when cut, bestows the drum's body, and how the sticks and rattles are taken, all to begin a new life as companions to the gods, music, and the dance. Bob Chilcott

Great Clarendon Street, Oxford OX2 6DP
198 Madison Avenue, New York, NY 10016 USA
Oxford is a trade mark of Oxford University Press

© Oxford University Press 1999

All rights reserved. No part of this publication may be reproduced, stored in a retrieval system or transmitted, in any form or by any means, without prior permission of Oxford University Press.

Permission to perform this work in public (except in the course of divine worship) should normally be obtained from the Performing Rights Society (PRS), 29/33 Berners Street, London W1T 3AB, or its affiliated Societies in each country throughout the world, unless the owner or occupier of the premises being used holds a licence from the Society.

Permission to make a recording must be obtained in advance from the Mechanical Copyright Protection Society Ltd., (MCPS), Elgar House, 41 Streatham High Road, London SW16 1ER, or its affiliated Societies in each country thoughout the world.

MUSIC DEPARTMENT

OXFORD
UNIVERSITY PRESS

Commissioned by and dedicated to Michael Smedley and the Oxford Pro Musica Singers on the occasion of their 20th Anniversary Concert, 22 November 1997

The Making of the Drum

1. *The Skin*

Edward Kamau Brathwaite

BOB CHILCOTT

* Rub hands together in rhythm (alternatively, use Sand Blocks).

Duration: *c.*12 minutes

In addition to SATB choir, the piece requires 2 Rainsticks, 2 Claves, 1 Shaker, a low-pitched Tomtom played with hard sticks (or a large Ethnic Drum), 4 Sand Blocks (optional) and Marimba (optional). If performance includes Marimba, the Marimba part is available to purchase (ISBN 9780193355378).

Text © Edward Kamau Brathwaite 1968. Reprinted from 'The Arrivants' by Edward Kamau Brathwaite 1973 by permission of Oxford University Press.

© Oxford University Press 1999

Printed in Great Britain

OXFORD UNIVERSITY PRESS, MUSIC DEPARTMENT, GREAT CLARENDON STREET, OXFORD OX2 6DP

Photocopying this copyright material is ILLEGAL.

8
mf
killed and the skin stretched.
First the goat must be
lall lall lall lall lall lall lall
lall lall lall lall
lall lall lall lall lall lall lall
lall lall lall lall
mf
First the goat must be
la la la lall la la la la lall la
mf

12
dim.
killed and the skin stretched, the skin stretched, and the skin
lall lall lall lall lall lall lall
lall lall lall lall
lall lall lall lall lall lall lall
dim.
killed and the skin stretched, the skin stretched, and the skin
la la la lall la la

* 4 singers clap.

* 4 singers clap.

* 4 singers clap.

39
skilled des - troy - er of goats; its sin spilled on the washed gra - vel,
skilled des - troy - er of goats; its sin spilled on the washed gra - vel,
skilled des - troy - er of goats; its sin spilled on the washed gra - vel,
skilled des - troy - er of goats; its sin spilled on the washed gra - vel,
43
ff
fff
dim. always
reach - es and spreads to de - vour us all, de - vour us all.
reach - es and spreads to de - vour us all, de - vour us all, de -
reach - es and spreads to de - vour us all, de - vour us all, de -
reach - es and spreads to de - vour us all, de - vour us all, de -

47
mp
Mm
dim. always
- vour us all, de - vour us all.
mp
Mm
dim. always
- vour us all, de - vour us all, de - vour us all, de - vour us all, de -
mp
dim. always
- vour us all.
mp
Mm
dim. always
mp
51
p
mm
p
mm
- vour us all, de - vour us all, de - vour us all, de - vour us all,
p
dim.
p
mm
p
dim.

* 4 singers rub hands together in rhythm (alternatively, use Sand Blocks).

64
mp
So the goat must be killed and it's skin stretched, its skin stretched,
lall lall lall lall lall lall lall lall lall lall lall lall lall lall lall lall lall lall lall lall
mp
its skin stretched,
la la la lall la la la la lall la
mp

68
dim.
p
and its skin stretched, its skin stretched, skin stretched.
lall lall lall lall lall lall lall lall lall lall lall lall lall lall lall lall lall lall lall lall
dim.
p
and its skin stretched, its skin stretched, skin stretched.
la la la lall la la la la lall la
dim.
p

72
lall lall lall lall lall lall lall
lall lall lall lall
lall lall lall lall lall lall lall
lall lall lall lall
la
la
la
lall la
la
la
la
lall la

76
lall lall lall lall
pp
la
lall la
la
pp

2. *The Barrel of the Drum*

90
rit.
a tempo
pp
with the hol - low blood that makes a womb. (mm)
with the hol - low blood that makes a womb. (mm) in this
with the hol - low blood that makes a womb. (mm) Here in this
with the hol - low blood that makes a womb. (mm)
rit.
a tempo
Rainsticks
1.
2.
94
SOLO
(like a sigh)
mp
(gliss.)
Ah
ah
ah
ah
CHORUS
pp
of the fo - rest; we hear the sounds of the
si - lence we hear the wounds of the fo - rest; we hear the sounds of the
si - lence we hear the wounds of the fo - rest; we hear the sounds of the
of the fo - rest; we hear the sounds of the
mp

98
ah
ah
mf espress.
ri - vers;
vo-wels of reed - lips, peb-bles of con - son -
101
p
SOLO
mp
- ants, un - der-ground dark of the con - ti - nent.

Rainsticks
1.
2.
106
mf espress.
You
p
oo
oh
112
poco stringendo
dumb a - dom wood will be bent, will be so - lemn - ly bent, bel - ly

115
f
ff appass.
round-ed with fire, wound-ed with tools that will shape you. You will bleed,
119
rit.
p dolce
pp
ce - dar dark, when we cut you; speak, speak, when we touch you.

3. *The Two Curved Sticks of the Drummer*

* Unpitched clipped rhythmic shout.

138
lull la la lull la la lull la la lull la la lull la la lull la la lull la la
bran - ches crack, crack like light - ning, like light-ning in the harm - at - tan.
hé hé hé hé hé hé hé
145
lull la la lull la la lull la la lull la la lull la la
SOLO
Lull la
(2.)
1.
lull la la lull la la
f
There is a quick stick grows in the
TENOR SOLO
Lull la
TENOR
There is a quick stick grows in the
hé hé hé hé hé hé hé

152
lull la
lull la la lull la la lull la la lull la la lull la la lull la la
fo - rest, blos - soms twice year - ly with - out leaves; bare, bare white
lull la
fo - rest, blos - soms twice year - ly with - out leaves; bare, bare white
hé hé hé hé hé hé
lull la
lull la
158
lull la la lull la la lull la la lull la la lull la la lull la la lull la la
bran - ches crack, crack like light - ning, like light-ning in the harm - at - tan.
lull la
lull la
bran - ches crack, crack like light - ning, like light-ning in the harm - at - tan.
hé hé hé hé hé hé hé

165
1.
2.
lull la la
lull la la
lull la la
lull la la
non div.
p legato
But no harm
But no harm
hé hé
But no
Tutti
hé hé hé hé hé hé
But no

171
comes to those, to those who live near - by. This tree, the el - ders say, will
comes to those, to those who live near - by. This tree, the el - ders say, will
harm comes to those, to those who live near-by. This tree, the el - ders say,
harm comes to those, to those who live near-by. This tree, the el - ders say,

176
div. 1.
mp
mp
1.
2.
1.
2.
ne - ver, ne - ver die.
lull la la
lull la la
lull la la
lull la la
ne - ver, ne - ver die.
(p)
_ will ne - ver, ne - ver die.
(p)
div. 1. mf
mf
2.
1.
2.
_ will ne - ver, ne - ver die.
hé
hé
hé
hé
mp

183
(sim.)
lull la la
lull la la
lull la la
lull la la
lull la la
lull la la
mf
From, from this stripped tree, stripped tree snap quick sticks, snap quick sticks for the
(sim.)
hé
hé
hé
hé
hé
hé
mf

189
lull la la lull la la lull la la lull la la lull la la lull la la
fes - ti - val. Its wood, heat-hard, its wood, heat-hard as stone,
hé hé hé hé hé hé

195
lull la la lull la la lull la la lull la la lull la la lull la la lull la la
as stone is tone - less as a_ bone.
hé hé hé hé hé hé hé

202
SOLO
lull la
lull la la lull la la lull la la lull la la lull la la lull la la
(Shaker 1 player)
From, from this stripped tree, stripped tree snap quick sticks, snap quick sticks
TENOR SOLO
lull la
TENOR
From, from this stripped tree, stripped tree snap quick sticks, snap quick sticks
hé hé hé hé hé hé
lull la
lull la
208
lull la la lull la la lull la la lull la la lull la la lull la la
for the fes - ti - val. It's wood, heat-hard, its wood, heat-hard
lull la
lull la
for the fes - ti - val. Its wood, heat-hard, its wood, heat-hard
hé hé hé hé hé hé

* Unpitched clipped rhythmic shout.

4. *Gourds and Rattles*

236
mf bright
Ca - la - bash trees' leaves do not clash;
trees, ca - la - bash trees, ca - la - bash
ca - la - bash trees, ca - la - bash trees,
mf bright
Ca - la - bash trees' leaves do not clash;
mf bright
240
bear a green gourd, bear a green gourd, Burn, burn
f
trees, ca - la-bash trees, ca - la-bash trees,
ca - la-bash trees, ca - la-bash trees, ca - la-bash trees, ca -
bear a green gourd, bear a green gourd, Burn, burn
f
f

* 2 singers clap.

255
sfz
crack o - pen seeds that rat - tle,
- la - bash trees, ca - la - bash trees, ca -
ca - la - bash trees, ca - la - bash trees,
sfz
crack o - pen seeds that rat - tle,
sfz

259
sfz
crack o - pen seeds that rat-tle,
- la-bash trees, ca - la-bash trees, ca - la-bash
ca - la-bash trees, ca - la-bash trees,
sfz
crack o - pen seeds that rat-tle,
sfz

264
sfz
crack o - pen seeds that rat-tle.
trees, ca - la-bash trees, ca - la-bash trees.
ca - la-bash trees, ca - la-bash trees.
p (menacing)
Blind
sfz
crack o - pen seeds that rat-tle.
div.
p (menacing)
Blind
sfz
p (menacing)
269
p (menacing)
Blind un-der-ground
p (menacing)
Blind un-der-ground
un-der-ground the rat's dark saw-teeth bleed the wet root, the rat's dark
un-der-ground the rat's dark saw-teeth bleed the wet root, the rat's dark

275
ff
p
bleed the wet root, snap its long drag of time, its grit, its
bleed the wet root, snap its long drag of time, its grit, its
saw-teeth, the wet root, snap its slow_ long drag of time, slow_ drag of time, its grit,
saw-teeth, the wet root, snap its slow_ long drag of time, slow_ drag of time, its grit,
282
cresc.
fla - vour; turn the ripe leaves sour, turn the ripe leaves sour,
fla - vour; turn the ripe leaves sour, turn the ripe leaves sour,
its fla - vour; turn the ripe leaves sour, turn the ripe leaves
its fla - vour; turn the ripe leaves sour, turn the ripe leaves

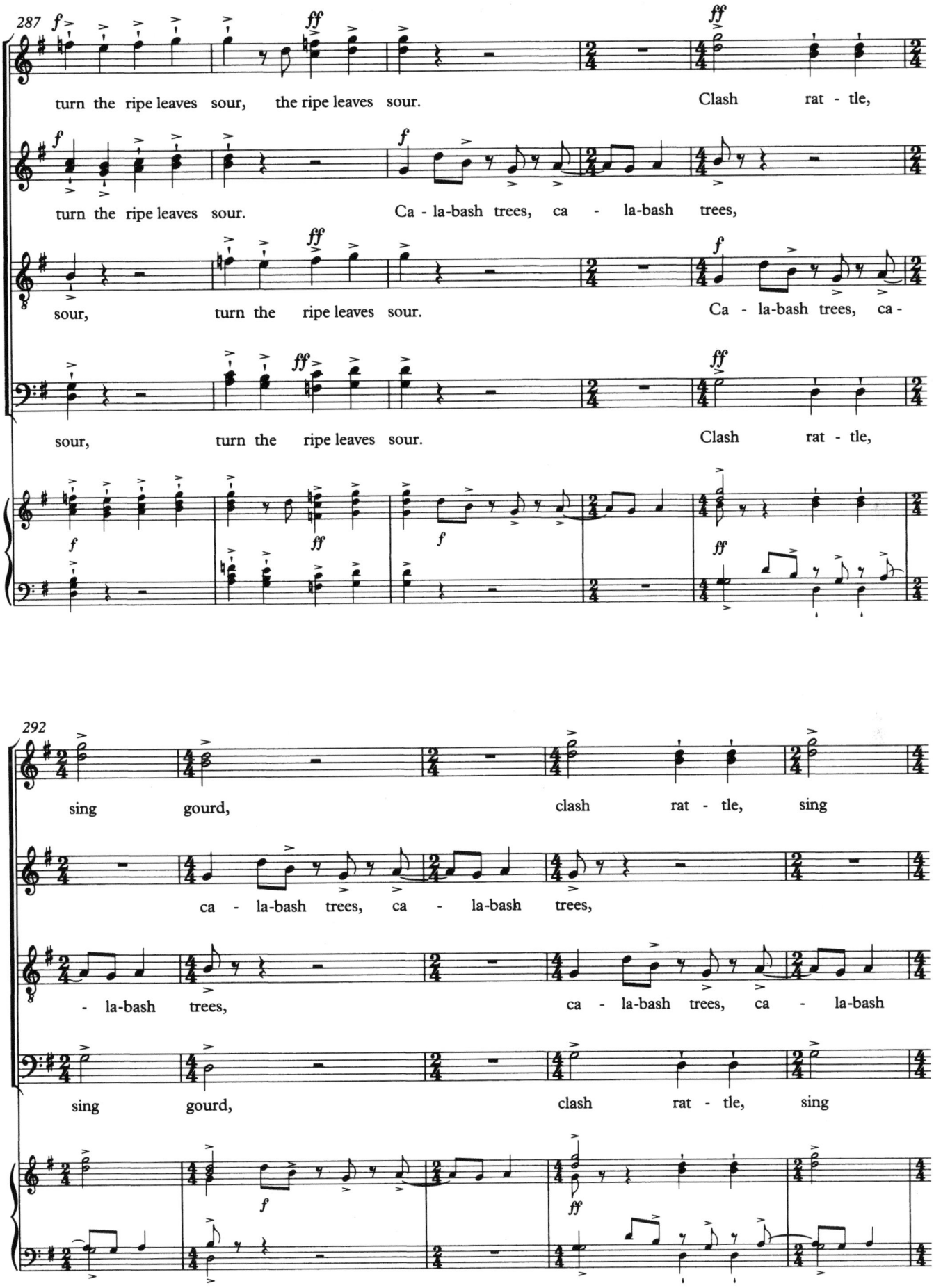
287
turn the ripe leaves sour, the ripe leaves sour. Clash rat - tle,
turn the ripe leaves sour. Ca - la-bash trees, ca - la-bash trees,
sour, turn the ripe leaves sour. Ca - la-bash trees, ca -
sour, turn the ripe leaves sour. Clash rat - tle,
292
sing gourd, clash rat - tle, sing
ca - la-bash trees, ca - la-bash trees,
- la-bash trees, ca - la-bash trees, ca - la-bash
sing gourd, clash rat - tle, sing

297
gourd, clash rat - tle, sing gourd,
ca - la-bash trees, ca - la-bash trees, ca - la-bash trees, ca -
trees, ca - la-bash trees, ca - la-bash trees,
gourd, clash rat - tle, sing gourd,
f
ff
f
302
clash rat - tle, sing gourd;
- la-bash trees, ca - la-bash trees, ca - la-bash
ca - la-bash trees, ca - la-bash trees.
clash rat - tle, sing gourd;
ff
f

307
f
ne - ver leave time's dan - cers wea - ry
trees.
ne - ver leave time's dan - cers wea - ry
ne - ver leave time's dan - cers wea - ry like this tree,
ne - ver leave time's dan - cers wea - ry like this tree,
311
like this tree,
ne - ver leave time's dan - cers wea - ry
like this tree,
ne - ver leave time's dan - cers wea - ry
ne - ver leave time's dan - cers wea - ry like this tree,
ne - ver leave time's dan - cers wea - ry like this tree,

315
like this tree and mocks mu - sic, that makes our mu - sic, that
like this tree and mocks mu - sic, that makes our mu - sic, that
that makes our mu - sic, and mocks mu - sic, that
that makes our mu - sic, and mocks mu - sic, that

320
makes and mocks our mu - sic, our mu - sic.
makes and mocks our mu - sic. Ca - la-bash trees, ca - la-bash trees,
makes and mocks our mu - sic, our mu - sic. Ca - la-bash trees, ca -
makes and mocks our mu - sic, our mu - sic.

325
mf dim.
Mm
mf dim.
ca - la-bash trees, ca - la-bash trees,
- la-bash trees,
dim.
ca - la-bash trees, ca -
mf dim.
Mm
dim.

329
mp dim.
mm
mp dim.
ca - la-bash trees, ca - la-bash trees,
- la-bash trees,
dim.
ca - la-bash trees, ca -
mp dim.
mm
mp dim.

333
p dim.
mm
p dim.
ca - la-bash trees, ca - la-bash trees,
- la-bash trees,
dim.
ca - la-bash trees, ca - la-bash
p dim.
mm
p dim.
338
pp dim.
mm
ppp
mm
pp dim.
ca - la-bash trees, ca - la-bash trees.
trees,
ca - la-bash trees, ca - la-bash trees.
ppp
pp dim.
mm
ppp
mm
pp dim.
ppp

5. *The Gong-Gong*

355
mm
p legato
p cresc.
God is dumb un - til the drum speaks,
God is dumb un - til the drum speaks.

360
mm
cresc.
mf
The drum is dumb, is dumb un-til the gong-gong leads it.

364
p cresc.
walk us through the
p cresc.
mm
walk us through the
p
cresc.
mm mm
walk us through the hum-ble
p
cresc.
Man made, the gong-gong's i - ron eyes of mu-sic walk us through the
p
cresc.
368
mf f ff
hum - ble dead to meet the dumb blind drum, the dumb blind drum, the dumb blind
mf f ff
hum - ble dead to meet the dumb blind drum, the dumb blind drum, the dumb blind
mf f ff
dead to meet the dumb blind drum, the dumb blind drum, the dumb blind
mf f ff
hum - ble dead to meet the dumb, the dumb, the dumb,
mf f ff

Printed and bound in Great Britain by Caligraving Limited